"As a pastor, I get asked lots of questions. I'm approached by unbelievers seeking to understand the gospel, new believers unsure about next steps, and maturing believers wanting help answering questions from their Christian family, friends, neighbors, or coworkers. It's in these moments that I wish I had a book to give them that was brief, answered their questions, and pointed them in the right direction for further study. Church Questions is a series that provides just that. Each booklet tackles one question in a biblical, brief, and practical manner. The series may be called Church Questions, but it could be called 'Church Answers.' I intend to pick these up by the dozens and give them away regularly. You should too."

Juan R. Sanchez, Senior Pastor, High Pointe Baptist Church, Austin, Texas

"Where can we Christians find reliable answers to our common questions about life together at church—without having to plow through long, expensive books? The Church Questions booklets meet our need with answers that are biblical, thoughtful, and practical. For pastors, this series will prove a trustworthy resource for guiding church members toward deeper wisdom and stronger unity."

Ray Ortlund, President, Renewal Ministries

Is Hell Real?

Church Questions

Is Hell Real?

Dane Ortlund

WHEATON, ILLINOIS

Trade paperback ISBN: 978-1-4335-7863-2
ePub ISBN: 978-1-4335-7866-3
PDF ISBN: 978-1-4335-7864-9
Mobipocket ISBN: 978-1-4335-7865-6

Library of Congress Cataloging-in-Publication Data

Names: Ortlund, Dane Calvin, author.
Title: Is hell real? / Dane Ortlund.
Description: Wheaton, Il : Crossway, 2022. | Series: Church questions | Includes bibliographical references and index.
Identifiers: LCCN 2022011784 (print) | LCCN 2022011785 (ebook) | ISBN 9781433578632 (trade paperback) | ISBN 9781433578649 (pdf) | ISBN 9781433578656 (mobipocket) | ISBN 9781433578663 (epub)
Subjects: LCSH: Hell--Biblical teaching. | Hell--Christianity.
Classification: LCC BS680.H43 O78 2022 (print) | LCC BS680.H43 (ebook) | DDC 236/.25--dc23/20220401
LC record available at https://lccn.loc.gov/2022011784
LC ebook record available at https://lccn.loc.gov/2022011785

Crossway is a publishing ministry of Good News Publishers.

BP		31	30	29	28	27	26	25	24	23	22
15	14	13	12	11	10	9	8	7	6	5	4	3	2	1

For God has not destined us for wrath, but to obtain salvation through our Lord Jesus Christ.

1 Thessalonians 5:9

The Christian teaching on hell offends unbelievers and is quietly avoided by many believers.
That is unfortunate because the doctrine of hell
is a vital part of living well amid the miseries of
this world. It may be painful for a patient to be
told he has a rapidly spreading cancer, but this
news is crucial for him to hear if he is to receive
treatment, get his affairs in order, and live his
remaining days meaningfully. Hell is not a fun
topic, but we need to learn of it, reflect on it
regularly, and warn others of it.

In this booklet, we'll look at what the Bible
says about hell. To summarize: hell is needed,

awful, close, and deserved by every one of us—but there is a way to avoid going there.

I wrote this so that you will see that hell is a horrifying reality. But if we are *only* horrified at the reality of hell, then we've still got work to do. A deep awareness of hell should also help us to live better lives than we otherwise would. And ultimately, it should swell our affections for the gospel—the good news that Jesus endured the horror of hell in the place of all who collapse into his open arms in trusting faith.

This book will not propose anything new. The teaching of this book, drawn from the Bible, is simply what faithful Christians have taught for two thousand years. I mention that because in our own time, the doctrine of hell has come under fresh scrutiny. That is, at one level, understandable. The thought of never-ending torment for the impenitent goes against our immediate natural instincts—instincts reinforced in broader culture by notions of the basic goodness of humanity and misunderstandings of the nature of God. But the widespread rejection of hell we see all around us, historically speaking, is relatively new. The generations before us have known the teaching of the Bible and of this little book: hell exists, and everyone deserves it.

Is hell real? Yes. But the hell that is there may not be exactly as you have envisioned it. And the real scandal of this universe is not that there is a hell, deserved by all, but that there is a heaven, offered to all.

Hell Is Needed

What's the first thing that pops into your head when you hear the word *hell*? Cartoon-like flames? Perhaps an image of people being gleefully and unendingly tortured, far beyond what they deserve? Maybe hell strikes you as one big overreaction on God's part. Or perhaps the teachings of Christianity are all plausible to you except this one doctrine about hell.

The first thing to get straight as we think about the Christian teaching on hell, though, is that the doctrine of hell is needed. It is healthy. It's even a surprising comfort to know that hell exists.

When I say "the doctrine of hell," I mean the teaching that those who do not repent of their sin and trust in Christ spend an eternity in conscious torment under the displeasure of God. We'll say more about what exactly this entails in the next section. But here at the outset I want to get clear in our minds that hell is not a problem. The *absence* of hell would be a problem. Hell is the affirmation that God is a God of justice, of fairness, of dealing with humans in a way that is right.

This is why down through human history and the many atrocities that have been committed by humans against other humans, it has been those who believed in hell who were most able to endure with nobility. If we do not believe in hell—if we think the only justice and retribution to be had is in this life—then we *must* take revenge into our own hands. Without hell, justice must be forcibly executed by us, or it will not be executed at all. If we wish to believe that God exists and loves humanity but that there is no such thing as this awful place called hell, life becomes far less stable. Any one of us might be deeply wronged at any time, and there's a good chance that we will be unable to execute justice, however savage our attempts might be. When a retiree is robbed of his pension by the corporate powers that be, and has no legal recourse, what is he to do? When a young person is abused and has no resources for legal action and no ability to secure any kind of equity, what is to be done?

Forgiveness itself, that beautiful Christian action that the world reveres, becomes elusive without hell. When the world torments and assaults believers, how are they to endure? How can I forgive the one who has hurt me without the knowledge that God will right all wrongs in the next life? The very act of forgiveness is founded on the notion that I am overlooking now what God will not overlook. "Beloved, never avenge yourselves, but leave it to the wrath of God, for it is written, 'Vengeance is mine, I will repay, says the Lord'" (Rom. 12:19).

So if we find the doctrine of hell hard to swallow, let's consider what we lose by abandoning it and what we are actually giving up. What if we all knew for certain that there was no place after this life where the impenitent wicked would receive judgment and justice? What if all wrongs were never righted but simply hung in the air of injustice eternally, never vindicated, never addressed, never brought out into the light? What if all wrongs against you were yours to sort out, before you die—not God's to sort out, after you die? That would be hellish indeed. And that is precisely how the world tends to operate and how many Christians wrongly operate—thinking justice must be exacted by them, in the present, not by God, in the future.

But calm and peace begin to break out in this world when we do believe in hell—when we settle into our hearts the comforting reality that God himself will right all wrongs one day far more precisely and justly than we could ever hope to do. This is a repeated refrain throughout the Bible—that God will not let the wicked ultimately flourish. Passages such as Psalm 73 and Jeremiah 12 show a man of God perplexed at the apparent flourishing of the wicked, yet in both texts the man of God comes around to believe afresh that God will "make them fall

to ruin" as they are utterly "destroyed in a mo-
ment" (Ps. 73:18–19). Passages like this may
not have in mind a full-blown doctrine of hell,
but we are seeing who God is. He is the kind
of God who, in his own time, brings judgment
and justice.

We can be at peace. We who know God can
hold our heads high and walk through this miserable world calmly, come what may. No matter how we are mistreated by the world, God
will bring perfect retribution and vindication in
his own way and time. God "has fixed a day on
which he will judge the world in righteousness"
(Acts 17:31).

God never looks the other way. He sees every
evil deed done in the dark, great or small. Nothing will slip by his omniscient gaze. We can live
in patience and in peace.

Hell Is Awful

But what exactly are we talking about when we
say "hell"? We hear the word used all the time
in a street-level way—"What the hell . . . ?" "Hell

no!" But when we stop and consider the actual reality of hell, beneath the irreverent and casual uses of the word, what do we find? In this section we'll consider what the Bible teaches about the nature of hell.

Scripture teaches us six truths about hell.

1. Hell Is Experienced by the Whole Person

A common misconception is that it is only a person's spirit or soul or mind that suffers in hell, once the body has been left behind. But the Bible's teaching is that while those in hell now are indeed suffering without a body, when the Lord Jesus returns everyone will be raised for judgment, and the impenitent will suffer in hell, *body and soul.*

In Matthew 5, Jesus twice speaks of one's "whole body" going to hell (Matt. 5:29–30). In another place he warns us to "fear him who can destroy both soul and body in hell" (Matt. 10:28). Humans sin against God with both their body and their soul; they suffer judgment by him, accordingly, in both body and soul. Some

Christians think only they are resurrected while unbelievers remain in a permanently disembodied state. But the Bible speaks clearly of "a resurrection of both the just *and the unjust*" (Acts 24:15; see also Dan. 12:2).

2. Hell Is Painful

We might hear our neighbors complain on a summer day, "It's hot as hell out here!" The crass references to hell we hear in everyday conversation shouldn't dull the agonizing awareness all believers should have of the pains of hell. Hell is where no sin is forgiven, where regrets loom large, where our folly and stupidity remain ever in our minds, and where God himself judges us with the pain that we deserve.

Some speak of hell as the absence of God, but hell is not the absence of God absolutely— indeed, it is the presence of God *in wrath*. The New Testament speaks of hell as a place of "chains of gloomy darkness" (2 Pet. 2:4), a place of "torment" (Luke 16:23) and "anguish" (Luke 16:25). We experience the judgment of God, and we are haunted by our many sins and follies. In heaven, all the sins and scars of this life become beauty marks that ennoble us all the more (Rom. 8:17–18); in hell, our sins and scars torment us. In heaven, joy squeezes out any opportunity for sadness. In hell, sadness squeezes out any opportunity for joy.

We should clarify one thing here. While hell is the presence of God in wrath, it is true to say that hell is the absence of Jesus. The God-man, Jesus Christ, is in heaven—as the ancient creed rightly teaches, Christ "ascended into heaven."[1] Indeed, Jesus Christ is what makes heaven heaven. There's a word for heaven without Jesus: hell.

Some object to Christian teaching on hell by saying that they cannot fully enjoy heaven if they know that they have loved ones suffering in hell. That's understandable. Human love throbs powerfully—husband for wife, parents for children, and so on. But here is what we must realize about heaven: we will be so overwhelmingly satisfied with God and Christ in heaven that there will be no room for sorrow. And that's not because our love for our family members in hell has lessened. It is simply because all earthly losses have been swallowed up in Christ and the love flowing back and forth between him and us. You do not mourn the loss of a penny through the drain when you have just inherited a fortune. Moreover, in heaven everything we love about our lost ones will be found in Christ, perfectly. Jonathan Edwards made this point three hundred years ago:

> When a saint dies, he has no cause at all to grieve because he leaves his friends and relations that he dearly loves, for he doth not properly leave them. For he enjoys them still in Christ; because everything that he loves in them and loves them for, is in Christ in an infinite degree.[2]

You don't mourn leaving behind your sandpit when you are going to the beach. While the damned endure hell endlessly, believers enjoy the endless perfections of Christ forever, and all that they love and desire is in him.

So, yes, hell is the presence of God—the righteous wrath of God, as unbelievers suffer the torments of their ruinous sin forever. A common image that the Bible gives us of hell is fire (Matt. 5:22; 18:9; Mark 9:48; Luke 16:24; 2 Thess. 1:8; James 3:6). This may or may not be a literal reference, but it hardly matters—the point is that the fierceness and heat and destructive force and fearfulness of fire are a picture of what will be experienced by those who spend an eternity in hell.

Yes, an eternity.

3. Hell Is Eternal

When the New Testament speaks of hell as a place of "destruction," that does not mean that those in hell cease to exist at some point, but that hell is a place of torment and chaos and breakdown. That's why Paul refers to "the punishment of *eternal* destruction" (2 Thess. 1:9). Scripture is clear: hell is an *unquenchable* fire (Mark 9:48). Jesus quotes the Old Testament to drive home the horrifying un-ending-ness of hell when he speaks of hell as the place "where their worm does not die and the fire is not quenched" (Mark 9:48, quoting Isa. 66:24). It's difficult to think about, but the image here is of a destructive worm eating its way through a body, while never actually totally consuming it—the body is simply perpetually gnawed on in a gruesome eternal torment. As the last book of the Bible puts it in describing the enemies of God, "the smoke of their torment goes up forever and ever, and they have no rest, day or night" (Rev. 14:11).

4. Hell Is Both Chosen and Not Chosen

This point is a bit trickier. Here's what I mean. On the one hand, all who go to hell have no one to blame but themselves. They chose it. Through hardness of heart and refusal to bow the knee to Jesus, through proud insistence on saving themselves and being their own lords, they willingly stiff-arm the free offer of forgiveness to all who acknowledge they are a sinful disaster and cast themselves on Christ.

This is reflected in Jesus's teaching on the rich man and Lazarus, which ends with Jesus saying that even if someone should rise from the dead, those alive on earth with hard hearts will not be convinced of the truth and repent (Luke 16:27–31). Impenitence is blind and hard and cannot be reasoned with. In a sense, the hard heart *loves* its hardness. C. S. Lewis captured this side of the truth in his imaginary depiction of hell in *The Great Divorce* when a character says,

> There are only two kinds of people in the end: those who say to God, "Thy will be done," and those to whom God says, in the end, "Thy will be done." All that are in Hell, choose it. Without that self-choice there could be no Hell. No soul that seriously and constantly desires joy will ever miss it. Those who seek find.[3]

At the same time, it is clear from Scripture that while the impenitent choose hell, God casts them there. God is sovereign over all, and he is not wringing his hands, weak and impotent, wishing fewer people would choose hell. The Scripture speaks of God's "authority to *cast* into hell" (Luke 12:5). Even the fallen angels are "cast" by God into hell (2 Pet. 2:4). If we do not repent we will be "*thrown* into hell" (Matt. 5:29). God is actively involved in a person's descent into hell.

We are now wading into a mystery that theologians call "human responsibility" and "divine sovereignty." Humans are responsible if they choose to go to hell. They have no one to blame but themselves. And yet God is supremely sovereign over all that happens, and he is the one who casts them into hell. The point is this: *both are true*. Our finite minds may not be able to resolve this perfectly. But we trust the teaching of Scripture, and we hold up both truths side by side, not allowing one truth to cancel out the other.

5. Hell Is Deserved

This is a clear biblical teaching, but because it raises all kinds of difficulties, we will hold off on this truth until the next section.

6. Hell Is for the Impenitent

We have been assuming this throughout this book, but let's close by making this clear and explicit. Hell is not for the worst people. It is for the *impenitent* people. By "impenitent," I mean someone who does not repent—that is, someone who does not acknowledge that they are a sinful wreck and deserving of judgment. "Penitent," on the other hand, refers to someone who has in honesty and contrition bowed the knee to Jesus and acknowledged personal wickedness, holding nothing back. The point is this: a penitent murderer goes to heaven; an impenitent orphanage founder goes to hell. That may offend you. But anything else is works righteousness. Christians believe the gospel, the good news that Jesus died and rose again so that anyone who believes in him receives full and free forgiveness. All our bad does not make us harder to save, and all our good does not make us easier to save. What saves us is Christ, and therefore all we contribute is honesty—admitting we are sinners and casting ourselves on him.

The world tends to believe that heaven is for the good and hell for the bad. Heaven is for those who found charities and feed the poor and pay their taxes and stop at red lights, and hell is for inmates and rapists and drug-lords and pimps. That is not the teaching of the Bible. The Bible teaches not that heaven is for the good and hell for the bad, but heaven for the penitent and hell for the impenitent—however good or bad anyone has been.

We'll return to the way to avoid hell in the final section of this short book. For now, we are simply getting straight in our minds: hell is awful. In Revelation 6, the impressive leaders of the world who do not bow the knee to the Lamb (Jesus) hide in caves and mountains and—consider now the fury of divine wrath—they beg the mountains and the rocks to fall on them, crushing them, rather than endure the wrath of the Lamb (Rev. 6:15–16). *That is how awful hell and the judgment of God upon the impenitent is.*

Perhaps as you think about the kind of person Jesus is, you have trouble believing he would actually endorse the idea of hell. But no one spoke about hell more than Jesus. We've seen some of his teaching on hell in this book. He returned to the subject frequently throughout his ministry. He had no hesitation warning the crowds of the horrors of hell, because he, more than anyone, saw the true frightfulness of it.

We cannot overestimate the horror of hell. It is experienced by the whole person. It is painful. It is eternal. It is chosen, and yet God sends us there. It is for the impenitent. And it is deserved. Let's consider that fifth point in depth now.

Hell Is Deserved

Hell is where God gives people what they deserve. You may think of hell as a place where people receive an exaggerated sentence. Can sin really be so bad that God sends people into an eternal torment? How can someone live for seventy or eighty years, die, and be sent to hell for billions upon billions of years, in never-ending misery?

A few things need to be remembered here. First, the key factor in any offense is: Who is the one being offended? If I deliberately step on a ladybug, that's an offense against one of God's creatures, I suppose. But it's just a bug. If I try to hit a squirrel with my car, that's a little more disturbing. If I attempt to run over a pod of dolphins in the Pacific with the prop of my boat—even more so. But what if I destroy another human being, made in God's image? That's an offense the ugliness of which can hardly be comprehended.

Now, take it one more level up—what if I hate and reject and try to destroy the Creator himself? That offense escalates even more than the difference between killing a ladybug to killing a man. For God is holy. Perfect. He made us. Perhaps you would object that you've never tried to "destroy" God. But isn't that what we all are doing right from the womb? Sin has sent us spiraling down into ourselves, and we naturally want to run our own lives and create our own self-exalting existences—in other words, we want God dead.

The second thing to remember is that no one who ever lived across the centuries of human history will receive injustice from God. Some will receive mercy. The rest will receive justice. No one is ever treated by God unfairly.

Let me state this second point differently. Ask yourself what you believe—what you really believe, in your gut—you deserve. Is it not quite easy to slip into thinking that we deserve heaven? That maybe we're not perfect, but heaven certainly seems more fitting for our lives than hell? That to go to hell would be unjust? Don't we tend to compare ourselves to others? Maybe we've never been to prison, always paid our taxes, and stick to the speed limit—pretty much, anyway. We go to church most Sundays, unlike our next-door neighbors. We say "thank you" and "please" to the waitress. We don't get drunk, we're not addicted to heroin, and we got decent grades in school.

It's really easy, as we look out horizontally, to feel that heaven is actually a pretty fitting place for us to end up. The trouble is that as long as we're looking out horizontally, we're not looking up vertically. And that's the view that shows us who we really are. Jesus told the parable of the

Pharisee and the tax collector to highlight this distinction:

> He also told this parable to some who trusted in themselves that they were righteous, and treated others with contempt: "Two men went up into the temple to pray, one a Pharisee and the other a tax collector. The Pharisee, standing by himself, prayed thus: 'God, I thank you that I am not like other men, extortioners, unjust, adulterers, or even like this tax collector. I fast twice a week; I give tithes of all that I get.' But the tax collector, standing far off, would not even lift up his eyes to heaven, but beat his breast, saying, 'God, be merciful to me, a sinner!' I tell you, this man went down to his house justified, rather than the other." (Luke 18:9–14)

The Pharisee, honored and respected by the people, compared himself to others, and did not see his true condition. The tax collector, hated and reviled for his immoral dealings with the

Jews, looked up and saw his true condition, and received divine forgiveness.

God is perfectly holy, supremely beautiful and pure and radiant. In him there is nothing ugly or cruel or bent. When he revealed himself to Isaiah, the seraphim (magnificent angelic beings) were crying out, "Holy, holy, holy, is the LORD of hosts!" (Isa. 6:3). Nowhere else in all the Bible is God given this kind of threefold repeated refrain. We're never told "compassionate, compassionate, compassionate, is the Lord," for example. His holiness is his supreme Godness, his utter deity—everything that makes him other than his fallen creatures.

And when we compare ourselves to *him*—then we realize we deserve hell. Have you ever wiped down your windows with Windex, only to have the angle of the sun come pouring through those windows a few hours later? What looked quite clean when only your bedroom lamp was shining is now revealed to be crisscrossed with smudges and remaining dirtiness.

That's what Isaiah experienced. He suddenly saw himself next to the supremely holy Lord—

and he cried out, "Woe is me! For I am lost; for I am a man of unclean lips" (Isa. 6:5).

When we look up and see God for who he is as perfectly holy, we immediately see not only who he is but who we are—utterly sinful. This is what Peter experienced in Luke's Gospel. Jesus told him to put down his nets after a night of catching no fish, and they immediately caught so many fish that the nets were breaking. Peter did not respond by jumping up and clapping Jesus on the back. He "fell down at Jesus' knees, saying, 'Depart from me, for I am a sinful man, O Lord'" (Luke 5:8).

We tend to think that the default destiny of all people is heaven, and hell is reserved for the particularly wicked. But in truth our default destiny is hell, and heaven is reserved for those who have the honesty to admit it and look to Christ.

Think of the difference between a window and a mirror. Both are pieces of glass, created to be looked at. But a window is looked through while a mirror reflects back and shows us ourselves. We naturally look out at others like looking through a window, but seeing God is like being given a mirror. We see ourselves. We stop comparing with other people.

As we ponder God's perfect truthfulness in Scripture, we are confronted with the many ways, subtle and unnoticed by others around us, that we spin the truth or speak in ways that make us look just a little better than we actually are. As we consider God's perfect faithfulness, we are brought face-to-face with the many ways we fail to keep our promises. As we reflect on God's perfect joy, we are rebuked at our own miserable joylessness beneath our perfunctory smiles. The candle flame of our goodness might burn a little brighter than the flicker of our friends or neighbors. But held up in comparison to the light of the risen sun, we see how small and inferior we are. And how ludicrous if our candle flames wanted to outshine the sun.

Scripture is clear: "The hearts of the children of man are full of evil, and madness is in their hearts while they live" (Eccles. 9:3). We have broken God's law—every rule of his in Scripture, we have, at least in our hearts if not in our actions, broken (Matt. 5:21–48). And we have not only broken God's law, we have broken his heart—we have held up the created things of food, drink, sex, and ambition, trusting in them for our deepest security and happiness rather than in God. In other words, we are idolaters. Both in terms of our lawbreaking and in terms of our idolatry, we know deep down—when we look up and compare ourselves to the infinitely resplendent Creator—that hell is deserved.

Hell Is Close

Hell is close because life is short.

It doesn't feel that way. We live in a world that bombards us with messaging that draws our hearts down from heaven toward the things of this world. The multi-billion dollar advertising industry fixes our gaze on how to enjoy this life, not prepare for the next, as they put before us one empty promise after another, that the right facial cream or financial advisor or pickup truck will deliver the longings of our hearts. Even Christian leaders reinforce the message that if we just have enough faith we can live our best life now, and even those leaders whose message is pure may betray that message through an extravagant lifestyle, showing us with their actions where their hearts really lie.

Thankfully, the Bible plunges through all the clutter and the noise and tells us that we'll all be dead soon. "What is your life? For you are a mist that appears for a little time and then vanishes" (James 4:14). The Bible looks with sober-minded realism at mankind and "the few days of his life" (Eccles. 5:18). Only fools ignore their looming death. "The living know that they will die" (Eccles. 9:5). The Bible is earthy and realistic in recognizing the inevitability of death and the sorrow that surrounds it: "It is better to go to the house of mourning than to go to the house of feasting, for this is the end of all mankind, and the living will lay it to heart" (Eccles. 7:2).

What about you? Do the eternal realities of heaven and hell seem urgently close to you? Do you ponder the reality that today you are one day closer to one or the other than you were yesterday? And that tomorrow you inch forward yet again? Unlike our movies and video games, we can't hit pause on life. God set the day of our birth, and God has set the day of our death (Ps. 139:16; Eccles. 7:17; Matt. 6:27). The only question is: Are we mindfully preparing for eternity? Or has the world successfully hypnotized our hearts into living as if we will never die, despite knowing in our minds that this is not true?

All this is sobering and solemnizing for those of us who will live a long life. Hell and heaven, one or the other, is inevitably hurtling at us, and it will be here before we know it. But what is really unsettling is that some of us will not live a long life. For some of us, death will come without any warning. That is the point of Jesus's parable of the rich fool, who built up a massive real estate fortune and thought to himself, "'Soul, you have ample goods laid up for many years; relax, eat, drink, be merry.' But God said to him, 'Fool! This night your soul is required of you'" (Luke 12:19–20). Jonathan Edwards once preached a sermon en-titled, "Youth Is Like a Flower That Is Cut Down" in which he sought to instill in his congregation a more acute awareness of the possibility of dying young. Perhaps that seems like a greater danger then than now, since we live in the age of modern medicine. But, of course, ours is also the age of heroin overdoses, skiing accidents, car crashes due to texting while driving, and a hundred other ways young people are taken to the grave.

Others of us may not be young, but perhaps we are in mid-life or our later years, and yet we too hold death at arm's length. Whether young or old, God loves us enough to tell us plainly in Scripture, with merciful forthrightness, that death may come at any time for any of us.

> The righteous man perishes,
>> and no one lays it to heart;
> devout men are taken away,
>> while no one understands. (Isa. 57:1)

It is not morbid but healthy to ponder your death. Perhaps you are a believer and not headed for hell but for heaven. It is still a salutary exercise to daily ponder the reality of hell. Look at it this way. Most readers of this book are a car-ride away from a graveyard. Within a short drive of everyone reading this book is a hospital or a hospicecare facility to ease the discomfort of the dying. Men and women are slipping into the permanent sleep of death and dropping into hell *all around us*. More than likely, in the next few days, within a few miles of the spot where you are sitting right now, someone will descend into hell. And that will be a tragedy that is utterly irreversible: "a great chasm has been fixed" between earth and hell, Jesus taught, "in order that those who would pass from here to you may not be able, and none may cross from there to us" (Luke 16:26).

Even if our own soul has been rescued from the horrifying destination of hell that we deserve, we still live in a world where men and women are moving steadily closer to hell all around us.

Hell is close.

Hell Is Avoidable

The great surprise of this universe is not that people go to hell. The great surprise of this universe is that people go to heaven.

Even at this point in this short book, having reviewed the biblical teaching and reflected on the healthy necessity of the doctrine of hell, the reality of hell may still seem terribly unfair to you. Given the horror of all that hell entails, that is understandable.

But the most important thing to bear in mind at this point is that *there is a way out*. And it isn't hard. It's within reach. No matter what we've done in our lives, we can avoid hell. We're not any further from hell if we've lived a moral life, and we're not any closer to hell if we've lived an immoral life.

For unlike every other religion, Christianity does not provide step-by-step instructions for what we must do to avoid hell; it provides a Savior who endured hell in our place, if we will simply have the humility to admit it should have been us. The Bible does not give us steps to take or a list of duties to fulfill as if avoiding hell were like building a bunk bed. The Bible gives us a Rescuer. "God has not destined us for wrath," the Apostle Paul wrote to a group of believers, "but to obtain salvation through our Lord Jesus Christ, who died for us" (1 Thess. 5:9–10). We are to collapse into his arms.

The reason hell is avoidable has nothing to do with any injustice on God's part. That is, God does not allow some to avoid hell by simply overlooking their sinfulness. God does not wink at sin. He is God. He cannot act unfairly. He can only act in fairness and justice. The reason hell is avoidable is this—Jesus endured hell in the place of all those who wind up in heaven.

To put it differently, *everyone's sin is punished in hell*, unbeliever and believer alike. Unbelievers' sin is punished in hell in the unbelievers themselves. Believers' sin is punished in hell by Jesus in their place. On the cross, Jesus experienced the full weight of all the sinfulness of his people, funneling down onto him in an afternoon the horror of which we cannot fathom. As he endured the God-forsakenness we deserved, he cried out: "My God, my God, why have you forsaken me?" (Matt. 27:46).

This is why we speak of Jesus as our "substitute." Think of school. Just as students may have a substitute teacher for a day, a teacher who stands in for the day to do what the regular teacher normally does, so Jesus stands in as our substitute, bearing the penalty that we ought to receive.

Now we begin to see more clearly one more reason why hell lasts forever. The horror of sin, the defiance of self and pride in the face of infinite Beauty himself, can never be fully punished. If we have sinned against an infinitely beautiful God, then that sin can never be fully met. On the other hand, if God's own Son, the God-man, absorbed the weight of that sin, then he and he alone can absorb a sentence of infinite proportion.

That may be a difficult concept. So let me ask you this, if you are still struggling with how all the math works in a sentence of eternal punishment in hell. If God sent his own beloved Son into this world to suffer and die, offering heaven freely to all who will repent and trust in him, is that not proof enough that we can trust God even when we don't understand his ways perfectly? As Abraham said to God, "Shall not the Judge of all the earth do what is just?" (Gen. 18:25). The answer to that rhetorical question is *yes*. Even when we do not understand God's ways—whether with regard to the Bible's teaching on hell, or a painful circumstance that has flooded our life, or whatever—we can trust him. He proved, in his Son's death, what kind of God he is. He put to rest all questions and doubts about his fairness. We can live in calm and confidence when we look to the cross.

What we are talking about in this brief final section is the good news, the best news, the most astonishing announcement that has ever been made or ever will be made in the history of the world. You can avoid hell. Anyone can avoid hell. Heaven is not for the deserving. It is for the repentant. Hell is not for the undeserving. It is for the unrepentant. As I've heard my dad say, hell is filled with people who think they should be in heaven; heaven is filled with people who know they should be in hell. Heaven is not for the obedient but the honest. Hell is not for the disobedient but for those who have not faced themselves, who refused to acknowledge that they are rebels against their Creator. They may have been upstanding citizens who got straight A's in school, cut their neighbor's grass once in a while, and gave money to charities. It is good that they did those things. But the final verdict over their lives is dependent solely on what they did with Jesus. Did they acknowledge that they need his death to stand in for what they deserve? Or did they simply view themselves as not as bad as others around them?

Some object to the Bible's teaching on hell by asserting that the way to avoid hell is too exclusive. *Surely*, the argument goes, *if hell were as bad as the Bible teaches, God would not have given people just one way out through Jesus? Is it really fair that sincere followers of other religions go to the same hell that serial killers do?*

Let me respond to this objection with an analogy. If you were on death row for committing a series of horrific crimes, and full exoneration were offered to you if you would simply receive it by acknowledging that you were indeed guilty—would you object that some other way out of your guilt had not been provided? How arrogant of us to demand another way, when full acquittal has been offered to us!

The astonishing surprise at the heart of the universe is not that there is only one way to get to heaven. The astonishing surprise is that there is any way to get to heaven for miserable sinners such as us.

Hell is avoidable.

Praise God.

Notes

1. The quote is from the Apostles' Creed.
2. Jonathan Edwards, *The Works of Jonathan Edwards: The "Miscellanies," a–500*, ed. Thomas A. Schafer, vol. 13 (New Haven, CT: Yale University Press, 1994), 167.
3. C. S. Lewis, *The Great Divorce* (New York: Touchstone, 1974), 72.

Scripture Index

IX 9Marks

Building Healthy Churches

9Marks exists to equip church leaders with a biblical vision and practical resources for displaying God's glory to the nations through healthy churches.

To that end, we want to see churches characterized by these nine marks of health:

1. Expositional Preaching
2. Gospel Doctrine
3. A Biblical Understanding of Conversion and Evangelism
4. Biblical Church Membership
5. Biblical Church Discipline
6. A Biblical Concern for Discipleship and Growth
7. Biblical Church Leadership
8. A Biblical Understanding of the Practice of Prayer
9. A Biblical Understanding and Practice of Missions

Find all our Crossway titles and other resources at 9Marks.org.

IX 9Marks Church Questions

Providing ordinary Christians with sound and accessible biblical teaching by answering common questions about church life.

For more information, visit crossway.org.